DON'T

MESS WITH ME!

Who Do You Think You Are?

GOD HAS A PLAN AND PURPOSE FOR YOU!

Poetic Messages,
Special Bible Scriptures,
and
Inspirational Articles.

WANDA J. BURNSIDE

DON'T MESS WITH ME!
Who Do You Think You Are?
Copyright 2013 By Wanda J. Burnside

PUBLISHED BY
Write the Vision Ministries and Media Productions Int'l
P.O. Box 125
Dearborn, MI 48121- 0125
Email Address: wtvision@hotmail.com
Website: www.thecalledandreadywriters.org
Phone: 313-491-3504

Book cover and page design by Shannon Crowley,
Treasure Image & Publishing - TreasureImagePublishing.com

Editorial Development by Minister Mary D. Edwards,
Leaves of Gold Consulting, LLC- LeavesOfGoldConsulting.com

CONTENTS

"I will praise thee; for I am
fearfully and wonderfully *made..."*
(Psalm 139:14 KJV).

Dear God,

"I praise you because you made me in

an amazing and wonderful way.

What you have done is wonderful.

I know this very well"

(Psalm 139:15 NCV).

You are a precious child of God.

God has a plan and purpose for your life. He loves you with an everlasting love.

You might be going through all kinds of things in your life, but you can make it through. God cares about you. You can have victory in Jesus!

"Nay, in all these things we are more than conquerors

through Him that loved us"

(Romans 8:37 21st Century KJV).

DEDICATION

This book is dedicated

In Loving Memory of my dearly beloved parents,

Elder Minor Palm, Jr. & Evangelist Willie Lee McCann Palm.

I am on this journey because of their faithful prayers, godly training, rich words of wisdom, and unfailing love.

*Mama, I am fulfilling your warning to me to **"never forget women's needs and ministries."***

Acknowledgments

I praise the Lord for my devoted and supportive husband, **Mr. Simmie Lee Burnside, Jr.,** who faithfully stands by me in the godly call to minister to others. Honey, since we were married in 1972, you have allowed me to seek after the deeper depths of God. You give me space and time to discover what God's plans are for my life. You generously make provisions for me to grow in the ministries that God has called me to do. I am thankful that you encourage and inspire me to fulfill them. I love and appreciate you! You mean everything to me. God gave me a companion who covers me spiritually and provides patience in all seasons of life. When I feel weak and faint, I am so thankful that God has made you strong and steadfast.

To my editor, **Minister Mary Edwards,** it is with much gratitude that I thank you for your invaluable services and professional help with this book. You have always been a blessing in my life since we met in 1999. We have been on a journey and have walked through many things together. I am grateful for your prayers, encouragement, godly instructions, support, knowledge, and friendship.

As president of The Called and Ready Writers, an outstanding writing ministry that you founded in 1999, I am thankful for a platform to work with writers. I am also blessed by the opportunities to advance in all areas of my own writing ministries. Thank you.

To **Miss Shannon Crowley,** the founder, owner, publisher of Treasure Image and Publishing, I am grateful for your exceptional and dependable services. Thank you for accepting this project to help produce this ministry book. God has given you a heart of compassion and concern for writers and authors. I sincerely appreciate your diligence and perseverance in managing the production of my book. You are spiritually anointed, skillful in your craft and have a vast insight in how to present only superior work that gives glory to God. I rejoice in the day that Minister Edwards brought you into my life and ministries.

To my great spiritual father: Bishop Earl J. Wright, Sr.: Pastor, Greater Miller Memorial Church of God in Christ in Warren, MI; Jurisdictional Bishop, The Second Ecclesiastical Jurisdiction Southwest Michigan Church of God in Christ, Inc. I am thankful for your many years of anointed preaching and teaching of the gospel of Jesus Christ. You never have compromised the truth. I am grateful for your years of prayer and concerns. It has been an honor to serve in your ministries.

To my pastor's wife and the Jurisdictional Supervisor of Japan - Church of God in Christ, Inc.**: Mother Robin L. Wright** - God bless you. May He always bless you to be triumphant and victorious in all your ministries and endeavors.

To my sweet-sweet greatly loved sister**, Ms. Regina Morna Palm.** You have always encouraged me to write and have supported my efforts. You have been an inspiration to me in ways you will never know. I am so very, very blessed to have a sweet sister like you.

Through the years, you have done all that you can to be there for me. You have stood by me with true love and concerns. You are truly so loving.

Regina, you live with tremendous faith in God. I learn by your walk of faith. You have made me better!

To my precious brother **Elder Rodger Minor Palm** and his devoted wife **Mrs. Josefa Palm.** Their family: Jason, his wife Stacey and their children Ja'Den and Jamisha. Julian, his wife Kai and their son Justus. Jolayna Lea Palm, Rodger and Josefa's daughter. All of you bring me so much JOY! Thank you for your love and fervent prayers. I love you!

MINISTRIES:

Thank you for standing with me. You have been there for me as I press on in the Lord. Your prayers have carried me through it all. You are a solid foundation in my life. I thank the Lord for my prayer warriors and supporters! You bless me! I love you so very dearly.

Pastor Michael Hands, Mother Elizabeth Hands and the members of SION National COGIC
Superintendent Willie B. Toone
          and Mother Roberta Toone of Michigan
Pastor Karen Butler of Michigan
Minister Deborah Foster of Michigan
Minister Tarsha Campbell of Florida

Pastor Lindsay Kotoman of Michigan

Pastor Tonie Gatlin of Oregon

Minister Celeste Kelley of Michigan

First Lady Paulette Harper of Florida

Minister Towana Parker of Michigan

Minister Sandra Hickman of Australia

Prophetess Theresa Johnson of Georgia

Psalmist Dr. Naima Johnston-Bush of Tennessee

Author/Editor Donna Goodrich of Arizona

Author/Publisher Susan Titus Osborn of California

Evangelist Cynthia Clark of Michigan

MY PRECIOUS FAMILY AND DEAR FRIENDS

I am so blessed to have you in my life and heart. Your continued prayers and constant encouragement have sustained me. I love you so much!

Cousins: Ms. Darlene Gardner, Mrs. Michele Barnes, and Mr. Daniel Gardner

My aunt and her family: Mrs. Katie Holloway and family: Stanford, Hope, Lisa, Patrick, and Payton. Mr. and Mrs. Tony (Marcia) Washington

The Johnson (Palm), Burnside, Campbell, McCann and Jones Families.

Special Church Mothers: Mother Frances A. Curtis, Second Jurisdiction Southwest MI COGIC, Mother Mollie Whitehead, Mother Barbara Spivey, Mother Barbara Lee, Mother Ruby Combs, and too many others to list.

Mr. Bruce Toussaint and (Darling) Mrs. Carolyn Toussaint

Mrs. Carolyn McKie and family

Ms. Donna Mathis

Mr. and Mrs. Terry (Linda) Whitsitt

Mrs. Joann Bowman

Evangelist Vera Beauford

Evangelist Jannett S. White-Gaines

Playwright and Author Izola Bird

Elder Gregory Coles and Elder Milford Schofield

Mrs. Verna Kokmeyer of Michigan

THE CALLED AND READY WRITERS

To the Administrative Assistants: Author Ramelle T. Lee and Poet Yvette Wilburn. I sincerely thank you for your constant support and many contributions in my ministries. I appreciate your personal link to me through your own anointed ministries.

To the Board Members: Ms. Trudy Hansberry, Chaplain Rev. Marva Stafford, and Minister Rhonda Roberson.

To all the loyal CRW Members: You are my family of writers. God has united us together to work and write for the Kingdom of God. We have a personal interest in each other. I am grateful to have you in my life. Each one of you are very precious to me.

TO MY LAMP NEWSLETTER SUBSCRIBERS, READERS, and SUPPORTERS:

I thank God for you! I appreciate your loyalty, prayers and concerns.

I have a heart of gratitude for the Copy Center Staff at Staples in Dearborn. Especially to: Ms. Sharonda Fitts, Ms. Katie

Laiklam, Mr. Rashon Warren, Ms. Christina Caster and Mr. Jim McIntyre, manager.

I thank the Lord for the anointed women of God who are a very special prayer covering over this book. I am forever grateful for your invaluable interest and vital concerns for this mission. Thank you for keeping a steadfast watch over this work. The Holy Spirit moved through you to stand guard over me.

God bless you:

Mrs. Carolyn Toussaint
Editor/Author Donna Goodrich
Minister Sandra Hickman
First Lady Paulette Harper-Johnson
Pastor Karen Butler
Ms. Darlene Gardner
Author Ramelle T. Lee
Minister Charlestine Herbin

Introduction

It's said that if you put crabs in a bucket there is a good chance that none of them will get out of it. This is because as soon as one crawls up, trying to get out, he won't escape. One of the other crabs will pull him right back down.

Is this happening in your life? You try to move on, but someone is there trying to hold you back so that you can't advance. Is this happening to you?

There are people who don't want to see you succeed or have any success. They want to hold you back. They are in your life to see that you fall on your back. These are the "I told you so folks." They are looking for a reason to see you struggle and not make it. They are not for you. We must learn to not listen to them. Instead, speak boldly about the assignment that God has for us. We can press on knowing that God is for us. He cares.

There is a holy boldness that we must acquire. The Lord wants us to hold on to His Word and not listen to the talk of others. He has made promises to us. He wants us to depend on Him and trust Him in everything. Our life will change when we believe what He said and stand on every promise. We must have a change of attitude to make it. Believe God and hold on! Stand firm on the Word that He has proclaimed to YOU!

Life's Not Fair for Me!

Are you in a place in your life where everything seems so unfair? You try to make things better by doing this and that, but nothing goes right. Nothing is going your way. Nothing happens like you planned. You try your best, but you are only left with failed plans and feelings of hopelessness.

You cry out, "Why can't I be blessed like others? Lord, I'm hurting! Why do I have to suffer with emptiness?"

So, you believe that since things aren't working out your way, what is the use of trying and pressing on. You ask yourself, "What can I do to make my life better? Do I have to live a life of being cheated?"

When you feel defeated, like you just can't go on any further, there is hope for you. Right in the pits of hopelessness and the dark room of despair, there is a Light that is there. What lies ahead for you when you feel so cheated and kicked to the curb by life? Can things ever change? What must I do to get things changed around for me? Who can straighten out my life from ending up going over the cliff?

God has the only answer that you need to these questions.

Cheated

"The troubles of my heart are enlarged; O bring thou me out of my distresses" (Psalm 25:19 KJV).

All of my life, I felt like I had nothing.
I felt cheated.
I felt like nothing.

It seemed like my dreams
were like dust . . .
blown and scattered
here and there.
I felt like I had nothing.
I felt cheated.

My life seemed so empty.
My dreams were only dreams.
No reality.
I felt cheated.
I felt like I had nothing.

Others had it all.
But what about me?
I felt like nothing.

I had nothing.
I felt cheated.

But, one day, in my loneliness
and despair,
I looked and saw Jesus Christ.
He just appeared.
He was standing there.

He reached out to me.
I took His hand.
He lifted me.
He held me in His arms.
I gave Him my loneliness
and despair.
He softly whispered,
"I truly love you.
I care about you."

I gave Him my empty life.
He gave me eternal life.
Now, I have life more abundantly.
He came to give me life more abundantly.

Once I felt cheated.
I felt empty.
But Jesus Christ came
to give me life more abundantly.

Some think that I should have
done something more to receive
life more abundantly.
See, Jesus came just for you and me.
He paid the price just for you and me.
He gave His life so that we could go free.

He took my sins and shame.
He took my punishment on the cross.
He came to give me life.
I have eternal life in Christ.
I cheated death.
Now, I have life!

From Adversities to Victory!

Women, do you feel like your life is out of control? Do you wonder why you are facing tests, trials, illnesses, discouragement, and other problems?   Are you heartbroken over your marriage, your children, and other painful situations? Do you feel like you will never move forward in your ministry?

In life, we want things to flow with peace, happiness and success. We want good times, good health, wealth, and great things. We work to obtain things that we need and hope will bring us the best in life. Some seek higher education to advance. Others want quicker results or changes so they take special classes or training to achieve their goals.

Today, we are encouraged to become health conscious concerning our diet, daily exercise, physical checkups, and lifestyle. We want a good marriage with a beautiful relationship with our husband. If God adds children to our marriage, we want to raise an obedient child or children.

However, life is not that way. In life, there are problems, oppositions, struggles, disappointments, failures, heartaches, and woes. Things will come against our plans, hopes, dreams, and life.

Sadly, even in the church, some marriages are failing; there are cheating spouses and disobedient children. Many people are facing home foreclosures, unemployment, and many problems. People who look like the picture of health are facing extreme health challenges.

In the Bible, there are men who had great tests and tribulations like Job, David, Moses, Daniel, Paul, and others. They had a tremendous testimony and ministry birthed out of what they went through.

God also gave us examples of women in the Bible who had adversities. They had tests and trials. But, God blessed and delivered them! Their adversities did not conquer them!

Let us consider a few of them and their troubles:

A widow woman in I Kings 17:9-24 KJV suffered hard economic times and little food. Then, later, her only son died. *But, God turned it around!*

Hannah's (I Samuel 1:2-28 KJV) womb was closed. Peninnah teased her and made fun of her because she could not have children. *But, God turned it around!*

The Woman with an issue of blood in Luke 8:43-48 KJV had poor health, was sick for 12 years, and went bankrupt. *But, God turned it around!*

Ruth and Naomi, a mother-in-law and daughter-in-law, in Ruth I and II their husbands died. They became widows without finances, a home, faced aging, and loneliness. *But, God turned it around!*

Women, situations may be overwhelming and hard right now. You feel like you won't have a ministry, but God cares about you! David went through many situations, but he learned that God is faithful to deliver us. He said, *"Many are the afflictions of the righteous: but the LORD delivers them out of them all" (Psalm 34:19 KJV). God turned it around!*

Whatever difficulties you are facing, God WILL TURN IT AROUND! In closing, God turned it around for Elisabeth in the Bible who was barren but, in her old age, she became pregnant. Remember what the angel of the Lord said, *"For with God nothing shall be impossible" (Luke 1:34-39 KJV).*

You will arise from adversities to VICTORY! God will turn whatever you are going through around. You are headed to VICTORY in Jesus!

Don't Mess with Me!

For God said

I am

"fearfully and wonderfully made."

I am not yours,

NOT ANYTHING,

or nobody's slave.

Look, don't get in my face---

You better behave!

I have a call on my life.

I am somebody.

I have a divine anointing on my life.

In the beginning,

before the beginning of time,

God formed me!

He called me.

He chose me

to be blessed and a blessing.

He has a definite plan for my life.

I have a destiny!

Don't Mess With Me!

I am created to succeed.

I am shaped to perform.

I may fall,

but I will not fail.

I may stumble,

here and there along the way,

but I will make it.

My trials and tests

make me strong

and strengthen me to go on.

They make me the "real thing."

They give me experience.

I gain wisdom and knowledge

from every test, trial and struggle

that comes my way.

God said that I am

more than a conqueror !

I excel.

I advance.

I go further.

Don't speak words of doubt

into my life.

I will not accept them

for God has a rhema word for me.

Out of the storms in my life,

I see brighter days ahead.

I will make it.

I will do

those things that somebody said

I could not do.

I will accomplish great feats

in The Name of Jesus.

For "I can do all things"

because He empowers me.

He strengthens me.

You may call me

stupid and ugly

to my face or behind my back.

You may see me

struggling, falling and crawling now

and living in lack.

But no matter what happened,

or is happening,

I will survive

and declare that Satan's plans

are big fat lies!

DON'T MESS WITH ME...

for I have on the full armor of God.

I am on my feet.

I stand wearing the belt of truth.

I have on the breastplate of righteousness.

My feet are ready and fitted

in the gospel of peace.

I hold the shield of faith

and I will put out all

the fiery darts of the wicked.

I have on the helmet of salvation.
And I have the sword of the Spirit,
which is the Word of God.
I am always praying and watching.
I pray for the Saints,
my sisters and brothers.

I boldly open my mouth
and speak the mystery of the gospel.

DON'T MESS WITH ME!

DON'T MESS WITH ME!

I am royalty.
I belong to a holy
and royal priesthood.
For I am now a child of God.

DON'T MESS WITH ME!

GOD WANTS YOU FREE!
HE WANTS YOU BLESSED!

"If God is for us, no one can defeat us.
He did not spare his own Son but gave Him for us all.
So with Jesus, God will surely give us all things.
Who can accuse the people God has chosen? No one,
because God is the One who makes them right,
Who can say God's people are guilty? No one,
because Christ Jesus died,
but He was also raised from the dead,
and now He is on God's right side, appealing to God for us.
Can anything separate us from the love Christ has for us?
Can troubles, problems or sufferings or hunger or
nakedness or danger or violent death?
But in all these things we are completely victorious
through God who showed his love for us"

(Romans 8: 31-35, 37 NCV).

"For I know the plans I have for you," declares the Lord, "Plans to prosper you and not to harm you, plans to give you hope and a future" (Jeremiah 29:11 NIV).

God's Plans for You!

"For I know the plans I have for you, declares the Lord, plans to prosper you and not to harm you, plans to give you hope and a future" (Jeremiah 29:11 NIV).

God has plans for your life.
The Lord spoke and He said:

"I have plans for your life. Your life has been designed for greatness. I have made a way for you to succeed. I know what is best for your daily walk from now into your future.

"My plans are to bring you hope and success that will not fail. My desire is that you have what will bring you peace and not sorrow.

"I don't want you out of control, confused, frustrated or worried. I want you to receive bountiful blessings that overflow the top of your cup. I desire that your cup overflows all those low places in your life.

"I want you to have more than enough. I desire that you have more than you expect. I have a special plan for you."

"Now unto him that is able to do exceeding abundantly above all that we ask or think according to the power that worketh in us"
(Ephesians 3:20 KJV).

"Speak boldly according to My Word.
Trust me to provide everything that you need.
Wait for My blessings. Stand still and wait upon Me.
Allow Me to give you blessings that will satisfy you.

Hold out your hands. I will fill them.
I will give you what you need.

I have blessings that will empower you!

I have blessings that will elevate you!"

I Am the Am

I am your Way.

          Follow Me.

I am your Hope.

          Trust Me.

I am your Provider.

          I will provide.

I am your Creator.

          I formed and

             shaped you.

I am your Father.

          You are My child.

I am your ALL in all.

          I care about you.

I will equip you.

I will anoint you.

          I will keep you.

YOU ARE VICTORIOUS!
Victory and blessings are yours!

"Beloved, I wish above all things that thou mayest prosper and be in health, even as thy soul prospereth" (3 John 1:2 KJV).

Divinely Made

There are some things
and faces in my life
that should not be.
I cannot allow them
To take over me.

For my good, they are not.
They have evil plans and secret plots.
They will not rule over me!
For when I was born,
I was born free!

Their words are poisonous to my soul.
My life they want to take control.
Lord, rescue me from this mess
For without You,
I am not strong enough I must confess.

I was divinely made in the image of
The Father, The Holy Spirit and The Son
And in my life,

Thy will for me will be done!
I have a victorious and divine destiny,
No one will have the rule over ME!

Stop Messing with Me!

"Consider mine enemies; for they are many; and they hate me with cruel hatred. O keep my soul, and deliver me; let me not be ashamed; for I put my trust in thee" (Psalm 25:19-20 KJV).

To become who God has planned for you to become, you have to stop listening to the binding, critical, non-productive, and restricting words of others. These people are Nay Sayers. You have to realize that they are out for no good. Nay Sayers speak words of doubt and negative talk, desiring to prevent you from obtaining all that God has for your life. They want to limit and prevent you from moving forward. They have been assigned by Satan to speak against the plans and destiny that Almighty God has for you. Before you were placed in your mother's womb, God had His own thoughts about you. He knew who He wanted to create for His glory. He had an image of you. He saw you in the form, fashion, and way that He wanted you to come into this world and walk in His divine blessings upon this earth.

Nay Sayers, the people who have come into your life to say what you can't and won't do, want to control your destiny and godly purpose. Satan is using them to manipulate or falsely handle your life. They speak fear and not faith into your life. This is to handcuff you to their predictions about your life.

In the classic children's story, *The Wizard of Oz*, we find at the end of the story the reasons why the characters: The Cowardly Lion, The Scarecrow, and Rusty the Tin Man were branded with these names. Throughout their journey in that fantasy life, they were unable to function, live and be who they were supposed to be. Although the friendly and very positive girl Dorothy, the main character, entered into their lives and tried to speak positive words over them, those three other characters: the Cowardly Lion, the Scarecrow and the Tin Man felt defeated. They were captured in fear by the controls of the Wizard of Oz. They were emotionally in bondage and subject to his manipulation of his control buttons, as he worked them behind the curtains.

We come to find out that this controller, the Wizard of Oz, was nothing but a tiny man standing on a tall stool pushing buttons in their lives. Satan wants Nay Sayers to push buttons on your emotions, beliefs and life with their words. If we allow them to enter our lives, we give them authority and power to bind us up so we cannot accomplish and achieve those things that God has for our success, peace, joy, and victory in our lives.

Get an attitude and godly boldness. God doesn't want anything or anyone to control you and your life. It is time to become empowered to say, "*Stop messing with me! I take authority in the Name of Jesus. Satan, you have no power over my life and destiny. The Word of God is in charge of my life. I live according to His Words and not your evil tongue!*"

Nay Sayers

"The lips of truth shall be established for ever: but a lying tongue is but for a moment"
(Proverbs 12:19 KJV).

I am tired of hearing
what **won't be**
and **can't be done!**
For I am depending on
The Holy One,
to direct my life.
He will make everything
<u>all right!</u>

God promised
to bless me.
He promised to help me.
He promised to
bring me out.
I won't let in a speck
of doubt!

I am tired of listening to
the **Nay Sayers** talk,
for they want to balk
at what God
is saying to me.
They can't see
what He wants done.
In my life,
He is Number One!

I am sick of the
Nay Sayers.
They don't live in faith,
but fear.
I don't want to hear
what they have to say.

SO, GET OUT OF MY
LIFE TODAY!

DESTINED TO SUCCEED

Look at YOU! Did you take a good look at yourself in the mirror this morning? I don't mean looking in the medicine cabinet mirror in your bathroom while you were brushing your teeth. I am not talking about looking into the tiny compact mirror that holds your face powder. I truly don't mean the mirrors in your car either. You know, the ones you peek in to put on your lipstick and check your teeth for food particles stuck in them. I mean, did you take a good look at yourself in that long, full-length mirror in your hallway or behind your bedroom door? What do you see when you look into the mirror? How do you look to you? How do you feel about yourself? Do you like what you see? Do you like you?

Most of the time, when we take a good long look into the full mirror, we kinda don't like everything we see. Maybe we see too many flaws from our head to our toes. We find those bike handles around our waist, full hips, a big behind, a tummy that needs a tuck, or hairy legs that need a good shave.

Some of us might see a fragile body that looks boney and weak. You find that your skin looks flabby, shapeless. You look flat-chested and flabby behind. There is loose skin hanging on you. Then, among us, there are those who look into the mirror and blow kisses at themselves and do a little dance. This is because they lost weight, they had their tummy tuck or a good breast implant, along with a tight lift on their derriere. They happily fling their full head of hair around and around!

Yet, there are many of us who see wrinkles, scars, cuts, bruises, skin discolorations, old marks of wounds from urgent surgery or serious operations. They see a stomach that has lines of stretch marks that won't fade away after having babies or drastic weight loss. Some see a head of gray hair or thinning hair that once was a glowing crown of glory. Some faces show the years of worry, stress and fear. There are crows' feet around their eyes, unwanted wrinkles on their forehead, and laugh lines that are really frown lines around their mouth. Sadly, some see all the hidden scars and bruises from the horrible acts of domestic violence from a husband or boyfriend who promised to love them with all of their hearts. In the mirror, some find the evidence of the painful memory of accidents that they narrowly escaped. There is so much to see when we look closely into a mirror.

Daily, we are confronted with who we are and what we must face. Just to move forward can be so challenging when we don't see what we want to see. We sometimes just want to get back in the bed and pull the covers over our head! We don't feel like trying to deal with anything. We can't be like a turtle and go inside a shell. See, we don't have one. Yet, we do draw inside ourselves and try to stay away from others. We feel inadequate to face ourselves and others. We feel like we can't deal with situations in life. We become fearful that we won't measure up to excel at anything. We feel like a loser.

However, God did not create us to be losers, failures, unsuccessful or inadequate! The Bible says, *"I will praise thee, for I am fearfully and wonderfully made..."* *(Psalm 139:14 KJV).* God made you to be WONDERFUL! YOU ARE WONDERFUL! I AM WONDERFUL!

God wants to lead us into the place where we will excel and shine. He wants us to have all of the blessings that He has prepared for us to receive. He will use all of our hurtful situations, challenges, problems, disappointments, and ugly flaws to bring about what is best for us. He has a plan set for our lives. Jeremiah 29:11 says, *"For I know the plans I have for you,"* declares the LORD, *"plans to prosper you and not to harm you, plans to give you hope and a future."*

This all means that we were so carefully created by a loving God who wants the best for us. His plans for us were before our lives began. Before we were born, God made a perfect and glorious plan for each one of us. It is a unique plan. It is an original plan for us individually. No one is like us or will have what God especially has for us.

See, we are destined for great success! Our physical appearances only enhance who we are. Yes, it brings out a uniqueness about us that makes us qualified for whatever we are to do. This makes us relative to our assignment or task. We can soar beyond limitations! We can obtain whatever we must conquer or face.

WE ARE UNIQUE!

God doesn't want you limited. Don't allow anything or anyone to block you from obtaining EVERYTHING that God has for your life. You must see yourself beyond that vision in your mirror. Low self-esteem hinders God's plans for you. Feeling inferior to others will imprison your life. It is bondage.

Stay away from those who are critical of you! Their bitter words are POISON!

It will KILL YOU! Don't allow them to speak negatively into your life. Refuse to accept what they say.

Those who are abusive, critical, and inconsiderate are deadly to your identity and self-worth! Anyone who tears down your self-esteem are like the school and playground BULLIES who poke fun at someone.

THEY ARE DANGEROUS!

People who violate someone with horrible domestic violent acts are verbally out of control. They shout, *"If you* weren't so old!" "*Your nose is bent out of shape!*" "*You will never go anywhere 'cause you're ugly!*" "*You are stupid and fat!*" "*You are a skinny bag of bones!*"

It is true that "hurt people hurt people." STAY AWAY FROM THEM! Don't permit them to come into your life to belittle you. They are all about humiliating you, embarrassing you, and bringing you down to feeling like nothing.

God warned us that human beings "look on the outward appearance, but the LORD looketh on the heart" (I Samuel 16:7b KJV). Remember this! It will do you good.

In Genesis, chapter one, in the Bible, God saw that all of His creation "was good."

He saw the beauty, worth and value of it all. It was all tremendous and glorious in His eyes.

Consider the potential of some of His creations. There is a lesson in it for us. The tall fruit trees live through years of cycles changing from season to season. They grow to produce and flourish with a specific fruit like apples, oranges, pears or bananas. Little eaglets in their nest hatch out of their shells featherless and helpless. But, they will grow to become mighty eagles to fly with enormous wings to soar high above the mountains! The lowly fuzzy caterpillars creep along on teeny feet. They change from one stage to another until they victoriously emerge free from their cocoon to fly away as a beautiful butterfly.

God created you and me to produce great things in our lives like the fruit trees. Like the eaglets, we are destined to be mighty and soar high! Just like the lowly caterpillar, we will go through one thing then another in life. But, we will emerge victoriously and fly away to new heights! YOU ARE DESTINED FOR GREAT SUCCESS! Trust in God. Declare: *"I can do all things through Christ which strengtheneth me"* (Philippians 4:13 KJV). Yes, you can! Yes you will... in the Name of Jesus!

"Unto thee, O LORD, do I lift up my soul.
O my God, I trust in thee: let me not be ashamed,
let not mine enemies triumph over me.
Shew me thy ways, O LORD;
teach me thy paths,
Lead me in thy truth, and teach me:
for thou art the God of my salvation;
on thee do I wait all the day"
(Psalm 25:1-2, 4-5 KJV).

From Mess to Blessed

God wants you blessed. He wants you free from those who have been trying to manipulate your life by telling you negative and discouraging words. He is standing there waiting on you to come to Him. Let Him bring you everything that you need to be victorious! *"Nay, in all these things we are more than conquerors through him that loved us" (Romans 8:37 KJV).*

GIVE EVERYTHING to GOD

The situations, circumstances and people who have led you to this place of feeling defeated and a failure must be released from your life. Everything and everybody must be cast over to Jesus Christ our Savior and Lord. Let it go! Let them go!

> **"Cast thy burden upon the LORD, and he shall sustain thee; he shall never suffer the righteous to be moved" (Psalm 55:22 KJV).**

DON'T BECOME MESSED UP!

You can't spend time getting up into people's faces trying to convince them to stay out of your life and your way. You can't make them believe that you are determined to press on and go on. For it is not in what you say, but what you do. Prove what you mean by your actions with a good attitude and disposition. If you don't prove it through your actions, they will make you more miserable. You will be deceived or tricked by Satan to take revenge or try to pay others back.

Leave it all behind you! Release it!

TAKE A GODLY STAND

God wants you to take authority and power over your life through Him. You can do amazing things regardless of what others say won't and can't happen. Remember this, *"I can do all things through Christ which strengtheneth me"* *(Philippians 4:13 KJV)*. New Century Version of the Bible states, *"...because he gives me strength."* Yes, God will work through you to accomplish many things for your good.

INSIDE OUT MAKEOVER

When someone pushes the wrong buttons in your life, it's hard to love them back. It is really difficult to be friends with those who are out to hurt you. Those ugly words, negative thoughts, painful situations, and mean criticisms, you want to get angry. You feel justified for being mean and wanting to slap somebody's face.

An associate of mine was frustrated by someone who she felt was taking advantage of her on her job. She felt uncomfortable with her because she did not trust this woman's intentions for my friend to move ahead on the job. My friend expressed that if she gets into her face, she is going to slap her. I was shocked! I did speak with her about this action and the impact of the reactions that could come from all of this.

When we are faced with conflict and confrontation, we must cry out to God to take complete control over our lives. Ask Him to make you over and create a new heart in you. Turn it over to Him. He will take control of these situations and tell you what to do or not to do.

"And the peace of God, which passeth all understanding, shall keep your hearts and minds through Christ Jesus.
Finally, brethren, whatsoever things are true, whatsoever things are honest, whatsoever things are pure, whatsoever things are lovely, whatsoever things are of good report; if there be any virtue, and if there be any praise, think on these things"
(Philippians 4: 7- 8 KJV).

Get in Christ by staying in the Word of God. Read His Word. Live and stay in His presence in prayer. Live for Him. You will be empowered by Him!

DON'T HATE THE HATERS!

"Hatred stirs up trouble, but love forgives all wrongs" (Proverbs 10:12 NCV).

The people who negatively speak against you and are jealous about the blessings of the Lord in your life are Haters. Haters strongly despise or bitterly hate to see you moving ahead, pressing onward, reaching for the goals in your life, and having success. They are irritated and upset by seeing your life turning around.

In their eyes, you look beat, weary, and weak. It appeared that you were going down because you felt stuck in the mud of difficult circumstances, struggles, and hard times. Don't hate the Haters! Instead, make that crucial and life-saving decision to reach out to God and trust in Him to bring you out of these pressing times. Don't use your energy, strength, emotions and attitude to hate. This will block-up your life with bitterness and resentment toward those who want you to fail. The flow of the blessings of God will not connect or work in your life when you allow yourself to give into a bitter spirit.

Release the hateful, bitter and jealous people who are not for you. Let them go by, no longer associating with them. Refuse to provide your time and the opportunities for them to speak into your life. Become busy or occupied with those things or people who are positive, productive and doing something good in life. You may have to disconnect your contact with them by setting your own boundaries in what you invest your time in. Then, God will give you His power to walk with determination. He will lift up your spirits. He will lift up your head. You will find that confidence will arise within you. You will begin to feel lifted up in your spirit, thinking, and attitude. Now, you believe that with God, you will make it!

Don't hate the Haters! Let God enter into the situation so that He can do what He promised to do on your behalf and defense. Don't get into God's business and His way! Stay out of it! Humble yourself under God. Pray. Wait, watch, and see His hands move. Allow Him to be your divine, almighty attorney. He will take your case and work it out for you! He cares too much about you to see you lose this battle. *"Beloved,... For it is written, vengeance is mine, I will repay, says the Lord"* (Romans 12:19 NKJV).

When God is finished working on what concerns you, He will give you His answer and direction on what to do and say concerning those who are against you. We must allow Him to work on or deal with their heart and attitude. He knows the core source of their bitterness. God will show them the way out of their darkness to His Light. He might redirect them to leave out of your life just as He often did in the Bible when accusers came before Him about someone. He may show them their faults and own sins like He did concerning the woman found in adultery and placed before Him. Her accusers came to stone her, but Jesus considered the women and her accusers. He knew both of their hearts and deeds. He dealt with them both to bring about what is right to lead to righteous or godly living.

However, He might use you to confront those Haters directly concerning the wrong that they have done to you. He will lead and guide you to do this if this is the best for you and your peace. For God will only move in what is right and just. In His wisdom He knows what the end results will be. He sees what effect your actions and reactions will have on the total picture of your life. You must yield to Him so that He can temper and adjust your life for the perfect outcome. Remember Jeremiah 29:11b NCV: *I have good plans for you, not plans to hurt you. I will give you hope and a good future."*

God is working on both sides; your haters and you. He wants to bring healing, deliverance and wholeness into our lives. He wants to set the captive free! To all who are bound by hurt and bitterness, God wants us set free from bondage to live free in Him.

FORGIVE AND LIVE!

"Walk in love, as Christ also hath loved us..."
(Ephesians 5:2 KJV).

Don't look back!

Put away regrets.

Refuse to be bitter.

Forgive those who have hurt you.

"Let all bitterness, and wrath, and anger, and
clamour, and evil speaking, be put away from you,
with all malice: and be ye kind one to another,
tenderhearted, forgiving one another, even as God
for Christ's sake hath forgiven you"
(Ephesians 4:32 KJV).

LIVE FREE!

"Though I walk in the midst of trouble, thou wilt
revive me: thou shalt stretch forth thine hand
against the wrath of mine enemies, and thy right
hand shall save me"
(Psalm 138:7 KJV).

You can no longer allow Satan to rule over or control
you. Take hold of the Name of Jesus and live free. *"If the*

Son therefore shall make you free, ye shall be free indeed"
(John 8:36 KJV).

Be bold in the Lord! *"...Be strong in the Lord, and in the power of his might" (Ephesians 6:10 KJV).*

THE KEYS to SUCCESS

You will overcome the drama, mess, criticism, and negative situations that are blocking your confidence and progress when you...

"Trust in the Lord with all thine heart; and lean not unto thine own understanding. In all thy ways acknowledge him, and he shall direct thy paths. Be not wise in thine own eyes: fear the LORD, and depart from evil"
(Proverbs 3:6-8 KJV).

GOD WANTS YOU BLESSED!

"Fear not, little flock; for it is your Father's good pleasure to give you the kingdom" (Luke 12:32 KJV).

Don't fear anything or anyone who is against you. Don't allow them to capture or hold you in fear. For God, our Heavenly Father, truly wants to give you the very best. This is His greatest desire. He is overjoyed or thrilled to give or release all things that you are entitled to possess or have.

"Now unto to him that is able to do exceeding abundantly above all that we ask or think, according to the power that worketh in us" (Ephesians 3:20 KJV).

"Beloved, I wish above all things that thou mayest prosper and be in health, even as thy soul prospereth" (3 John 2 KJV).

EMPOWERED to LIVE!

"What shall we then say to these things? If God be for us, who can be against us?"
(Romans 8:31 KJV).

Follow the ways of the Lord. Live according to God's Word. Have faith in Him. The whole world might stand against you, but God will be for you. When He is with you and for you, He will empower you to live. You will have power and victory in your life. God will defend you. He will fight your battles. He will make a way for you.

GO YOUR WAY

In the Bible, when Jesus healed anyone who was sick or in bondage, He told them to "go." He was saying, you are now healed and delivered from this evil sickness, oppression, depression, and power of the devil. You are set free now to go and fully live your life. No more restrictions and limitations are in your life. I have set you free. In Luke, we find Him saying, *"Go your way"* or *"Go your ways"* in Luke 7:22 KJV and Luke 10:3,37. In other chapters in the Bible, He said, *"Go!"*

In the closing pages of this book, God has given me a special prayer for you. He has come to set the hurting and broken free. He is waiting to give you His wisdom. He wants to pour it into your life so it can operate inside of you.

His Holy Spirit will be released into your life. He, the Spirit of God, will give you a clear revelation of what is right for you. He will daily lead and guide you. He will comfort your weary heart and bring peace to your troubled mind.

God doesn't want you limited and restricted by people or things that are not for your good. He doesn't want you living in fear or lack. This is Satan's plans. It is not God's will for you to have a mind that is controlled by limitations.

It is now time to ask for and receive God's directions to the pathway for your life. He will set you free. Fully give your life to Him. He will transform or change everything that concerns you. You will be changed to possess His power and walk in godly authority. Trust and depend upon Him to bring you victoriously through all of the oppositions and struggles in your life.

GO! GO YOUR WAY! LIVE YOUR LIFE!

"The LORD is my light and my salvation;
whom shall I fear?
The LORD is the strength of my life:
of whom shall I be afraid?
When the wicked, even mine enemies and my foes,
came upon me to eat up my flesh,
They stumbled and fell.
For in the time of trouble he shall hide me in his
pavilion:
in the secret of his tabernacle shall he hide me;
he shall set me up upon a rock"
(Psalm 27:1-2, 5 KJV).

I Have Authority

*"And I will give unto thee
the keys of the kingdom of heaven:
and whatsoever thou shalt bind on earth
shall be bound in heaven:
and whatsoever thou shalt loose on earth
shall be loosed in heaven" (Matthew 16:19 KJV).*

God has given me authority!
I have dominion and power on earth.
I have been given,
the full godly right
to fully function and operate here on earth
by
the Spirit of God.

In the Name of Jesus:
I have the authority to give and speak
spiritual orders using the Word of God.

In the Name of Jesus:
I have the godly power and right to
enforce the kingdom of darkness to obey.
I have the official power of God.
Therefore, in the Kingdom of God

I AM:

recognized,

acknowledged,

and authorized to speak as God commands.

I have God's official permission,

and His approval,

to take authority and dominion

over all things.

I have legal entitlement to His provisions.

I AM:

approved

and

empowered

to live my life in abundance.

According to God's Holy Word:
"He that dwelleth in the secret place
of the Most High
shall abide under the shadow of the almighty"
(Psalm 91:1 KJV).

I can enter into the presence of God.

I dwell in His Holy presence.

I can abide with Him.

He abides with me.

He abides in me.

He is my hiding place.

He is my shield.

He protects me.

He covers me with His Spirit.

According to the Word of the LORD in Psalm 91:4b:

His truth is my shield and protection.

According to the Word of the LORD in Psalm 91:9-13:

He has put His angels in charge over me.

They watch over me wherever I go.

They will catch me in their hands

so that I will not hit my foot against a rock.

He protects and watches guard over me-

I can walk on lions and cobras;

I can step on strong lions and snakes.

He will help me.

According to the Word of the LORD in Psalm 91:14-15:

He will protect me.

When I call upon Him, He will answer me.

He will be with me in trouble.

He will rescue me.

He will honor me.

He will give me a long life.

Nothing can separate me from the love of God . . .

Who can be against me?

I can pull down strongholds

in the Name of Jesus.

I can speak in authority

according to the Word of God.

In the Name of Jesus,

I can declare that I am blessed.

I am the redeemed of the Lord.

I can obtain all of the promises of God.

For, "I can do all things through Christ which strengtheneth me"
(Philippians 4:13 KJV).

Mountains cannot come against me.
"No weapon that is formed against me
shall prosper . . . " (Isaiah 54:17 KJV).

Every good and perfect gift is mine!

Wealth is mine according to my obedience to God!

Blessings are mine!

Healing is mine!

Deliverance is mine!

Peace is mine!

Miracles are mine!

Joy is mine!

Peace is mine!

Salvation is mine!

A New Life is mine!

Forgiveness from sins is mine!

Redemption is mine!

Eternal Life with God is mine!

CLOSING PRAYER

Dear Heavenly Father,

I boldly come to You in the glorious and
wonderful name of Your Son, Jesus Christ.
I give You praise and honor
for all that You have done for me.
You are the Author and the Finisher of my life.
You are the Alpha and Omega.
You are the beginning and the end.
I praise You for all of Your many blessings in my life.

Thank you for the plan You made for my life.
I rejoice knowing that You care about me.
You are in charge of my life, therefore, You order my steps.

I have a definite path to follow.
I am not alone.
You are there to guide me step by step.
You direct me in the way that I should go.

My heart rejoices because You are here for me.
You speak over my life.

You declare the good news of what will happen,

if I follow Your Word and Your Way.

You warn me when I am out of Your will.

You provide all that I need.

You will change those things in my life

that are not for me.

You will show me how to come forth.

My life and time is in Your hands.

You watch over me.

You will protect me from Satan's tricks.

You operate in my life.

You are for me when the world is against me.

I thank you, Lord.

I praise You for protecting me

in situations that would have destroyed me.

I praise You for holding me in Your arms

in circumstances where I would have lost my mind

and done the wrong thing.

I would have said the wrong thing if you weren't there.

I would have missed Your plans

and the destiny for my life,

if I wasn't led by Your Spirit.

Keep me, Jesus.

I know that my walk with You

will be blessed and I will succeed

according to Your Word.

Thank you for preserving me

from those things

that would have come against me

to bring me down.

Thank you for helping me

in the time of trouble.

I put my trust in You.

I depend upon You.

I give You glory and praise. *Amen*

*"Wait on the LORD: be of good courage, and he shall
strengthen thine heart: wait, I say, on the LORD"
(Psalm 27:14 KJV).*

GOD BLESS YOU

May overflowing blessings and bountiful favor of God be greatly upon your life.

**[Jabez] "He was the one who prayed
to the God of Israel,
'Oh, that you would bless me
and expand my territory!
Please be with me
in all that I do,
and keep me from all trouble and pain!'
And God granted him his request"
(I Chronicles 4:10 KLT).**

Contact Information:

I look forward to hearing from you. You can contact me about my gospel tracts, books, ministry pamphlets, literary products, newsletter, and other items. I am available to speak, teach and minister at your conferences, retreats, revivals, and special events.

Please feel free to contact me at:
Mrs. Wanda J. Burnside, Founder
Write the Vision Ministries and Media Productions Int'l
P.O. Box 125
Dearborn, MI 48121- 0125
wtvision@hotmail.com
www.thecalledandreadywriters.org
313-491-3504

You can also contact me at:
Facebook, LinkedIn and Twitter

ABOUT THE AUTHOR:

Mrs. Wanda J. Burnside is an award-winning poet and writer. Since 1970, she has received numerous national and local honors in writing. At the age of 20, while a student at the University of Detroit, she received her first poetry award from Broadside Press. The famed Michigan Poet Laureate, Mr. Dudley Randall, who was the founder of this organization, awarded her with this prestigious honor. In 1999, she received both "The Writer of the Year Award" and "The Persistence Writer of the Year Award" from the American Christian Writers Association.

Wanda is one of the contributing poets in the newly released anthology, *SISTAHFAITH: Real Stories of Pain, Truth, and Triumph* published by Simon and Schuster of New York. This book was compiled by the noted author and speaker, Marilynn Griffith. Wanda is a contributing author and poet in other major Christian books such as: *Too Soon to Say Goodbye* and *Wounded by Words* true painful stories compiled by Susan Titus Osborn, MA, Karen L. Kosman and Jeenie Gordon, MS, MA, LMFT. *FAITH: Use It . . . or Lose It!* By Minister Mary Edwards.

She has written three books: *Rejections - 12 Steps to Recovery, The Christian Poetry Guide* and *Free From It!* Several new books will be published: *STAND, Deliver Us from Evil,* and others. She has written more than 1,000 poems, 22 performed plays for children and four drama productions for adults.

Her poems, *"A Prayer Can Reach Heaven," "Come to Me,"* and other poems have been produced as video productions by Webtech Design Group. These highly acclaimed videos have changed lives around the world with their inspirational messages.

Her articles, devotionals, prayers, short stories, and gospel messages are regularly published in magazines, journals, newspapers, and anthologies. Wanda's work is published on websites and online magazines with The Sistahs Ministry, WomenNPower, The Called and Ready Writers and many other ministries. She has received poetry honors, publication and recognition with The Roberta Heck's Ministry, Rhonda Welsh Ministries, and other leading ministries around the United States.

In 2003, her story titled, *"A Slice of Mama's Pie"* was selected as one of the prize winning stories in a special commemorative edition of *The Michigan Chronicle* and *The Michigan Front Page* newspapers for the "Women of Purpose" competition.

Wanda is:

The founder and president of "Write the Vision Ministries and Media Productions International." Since 1995, she has published ten gospel tracts with more than 8,000 distributed across the United States, Canada, Honduras, London, Italy, and in Africa (Zambia and Kenya).

The publisher and president of THE LAMP NEWSLETTER. It is a bi-monthly newsletter which features articles, poetry, inspirational messages, news, views, social updates, and other vital information. Lamp Newsletter was established in 2008. Her readership is worldwide.

The founder and president of "The Mother Willie Lee Palm Foundation," established to continue the legacy and vital mission of her mother to help the needy, support youth programs, and give monetary donations to charitable organizations.

The president and poetry editor of "The Called and Ready Writers" of Detroit, founded in 1999 by Minister Mary D. Edwards.

The administrator of the Café of Christian Books in "The Sistahs Ministry International" co-founded and directed by Reverend Celeste Kelley. She selects and promotes the work of authors and poets around the world.

Wanda was the editor and staff writer of *The Detroit Church World Magazine* in the 1980's. Bishop Floyd Mitchell was the founder and chief editor. She also was the coordinator and editor for the Marygrove College Course Directory.

In 1972, she graduated from the University of Detroit with a B.S. in Humanities/Early Education. Wanda has taught grades K-7 in public and private schools in the Detroit area. She also has tutored students in middle school and high school.

Wanda is certified in several Christian ministries from William Tyndale College. Wanda further pursued Christian education at Charles Harrison Mason Church of God in Christ Bible College in Detroit. She is one of their founding students.

Her parents, Elder Minor Palm, Jr. and Missionary Willie Lee Palm, trained her as a child to serve the Lord. She has faithfully served her church, Greater Miller Memorial Church of God in Christ. Bishop Earl J. Wright, Sr. is the pastor.

Wanda taught Sunday School for over 35 years, worked for more than 20 years in the Vacation Bible School Dept., served as the Public Relations Director for nearly 40 years, and other areas of leadership in the church. Wanda actively served in the choir, usher board, missions, and several other departments. She was Bishop Earl Jerome Wright's executive secretary for nearly 20 years.

Throughout the years, she has received many distinguished awards for church and community services. In 1990, The Congress of national Black churches presented her with "The Laity Leadership Award." The following year, in 1991, The Association of Christian Business Owners honored her with "The Founder's Award" for outstanding service to the Church of God in Christ by a Layperson.

In 1972, Wanda married Mr. Simmie Lee Burnside, Jr. He is a devoted husband and manager of "Write the Vision Ministries and Media Productions International." Simmie actively serves in various other church ministries. They live in Detroit, MI.

Made in the USA
Charleston, SC
02 February 2017